DISCOVERING PiRATES

Discovering PiRATES

Richard Platt

ReD KiTE

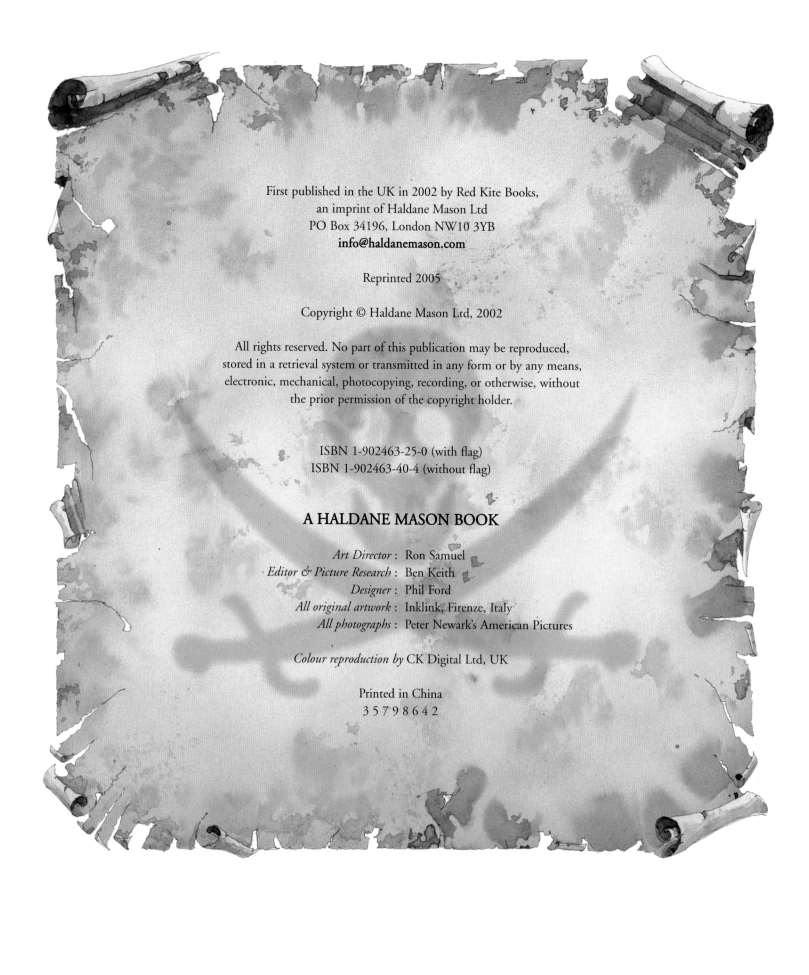

First published in the UK in 2002 by Red Kite Books,
an imprint of Haldane Mason Ltd
PO Box 34196, London NW10 3YB
info@haldanemason.com

Reprinted 2005

ISBN 1-902463-25-0 (with flag)
ISBN 1-902463-40-4 (without flag)

A HALDANE MASON BOOK

Art Director : Ron Samuel
Editor & Picture Research : Ben Keith
Designer : Phil Ford
All original artwork : Inklink, Firenze, Italy
All photographs : Peter Newark's American Pictures

Colour reproduction by CK Digital Ltd, UK

Printed in China
3 5 7 9 8 6 4 2

CONTENTS

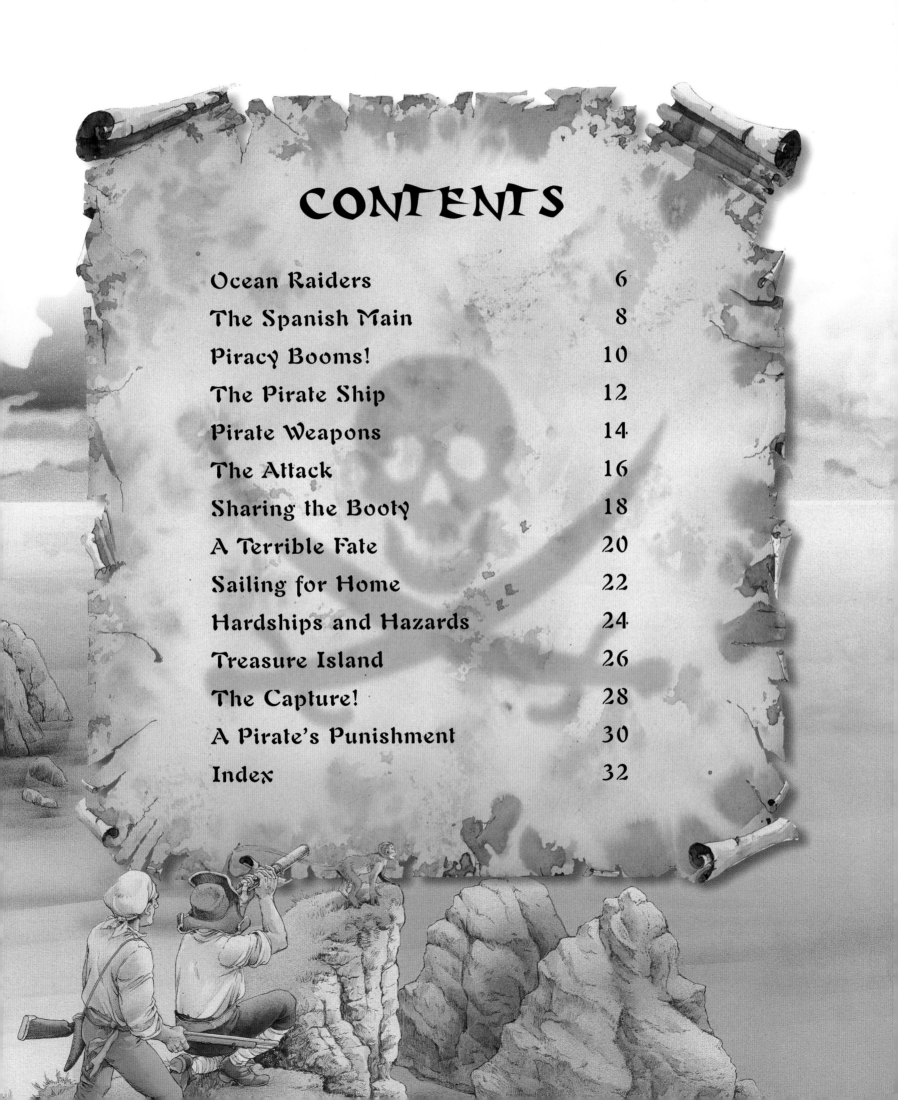

Ocean Raiders   6

The Spanish Main   8

Piracy Booms!   10

The Pirate Ship   12

Pirate Weapons   14

The Attack   16

Sharing the Booty   18

A Terrible Fate   20

Sailing for Home   22

Hardships and Hazards   24

Treasure Island   26

The Capture!   28

A Pirate's Punishment   30

Index   32

OCEAN RAIDERS

When the first sailing ships headed out to sea, pirates weren't far behind. To seize a ship and steal the goods it carried, pirates often murdered the crew, or captured them to sell as slaves.

The mariners of the ancient world braved terrible hazards. They learned how to steer clear of rocks and sandbanks that wrecked their fragile ships. They could avoid storms and huge waves by watching for signs of bad weather in the skies. But there was one hazard that the first sailors could not escape: pirates! Pirates are sea robbers. The first pirates attacked sea-going vessels to steal their precious cargo. When there were no ships to raid, some pirates turned to the land. They anchored on remote coasts and plundered ports and harbours. They stole the wealth of the villagers, carrying off the fittest and most beautiful children to sell as slaves.

▲ **A corsair:** a pirate from the part of the North African coastline known as the Barbary Coast.

▲ **An Assyrian galley:** a speedy vessel that could be powered by oars as well as sails.

Piracy began in the Mediterranean Sea, for it was here, 5,000 years ago, that people first set sail for foreign ports. The earliest sailors dared not venture out of sight of land and always stayed close to shore. This made them easy prey for pirates, who could simply lurk in a bay or inlet, waiting to pounce.

As the centuries passed, mariners became more adventurous. They learned to navigate (find their way across) the open seas, out of sight of land. They stuck to familiar routes, however, so pirates had no trouble in finding and raiding their ships. Pirates in fast galleys (vessels powered by oars as well as sails) raided the shipping of the Greek civilization in the Aegean and Mediterranean seas between 1500 and 350 BC. Even the Romans, who had conquered most of the Mediterranean coast by 75 BC, had trouble from pirates in what is now southern Turkey. Julius Caesar, later the greatest of Roman rulers, was held prisoner by pirates until his family paid for his freedom.

Further north, the mariners of Scandinavia made plundering a profession in the 9th century. They swooped on ships at sea and raided Britain's North Sea coasts. The name we use for these sea robbers comes from *vik*, the old Norse name for the creeks and inlets where they hid; we call them the Vikings.

◂ **An Athenian drinking bowl:** bowls and cups were often painted; this one shows pirate adventures on the high seas in the 6th century BC.

☠ THE BUCCANEERS OF HISPANIOLA

When Europeans sailed across the Atlantic, one of the first islands they settled was Hispaniola (now called Haiti and the Dominican Republic) in the Caribbean. When the original Spanish settlers moved on, people of other nationalities replaced them. They made a living by hunting the pigs and cattle that ran wild on the island. Passing sailors bought the meat that the hunters preserved by smoking over a grill called a 'boucan'. These rough hunters were named after their barbecues: they became 'boucaniers'. By 1600, they had discovered that hunting ships at sea was more profitable than hunting cattle on land. As 'buccaneers' they had become the first Caribbean pirates.

▸ **A boucan:** a 16th-century 'barbecue' that gave buccaneers their name.

'All aboard!' the captain shouts
 and beckons to his pirate band.
The master is the first aboard –
 he'll steer them safely clear of land.
The quartermaster, gunner, cook,
 mate and bosun report for duty;
With the seamen they will share the
 danger . . . and the captured booty.

THE SPANISH MAIN

For fearless or reckless 16th-century pirates, Spanish ships were the richest prizes. They carried tons of gold and silver looted from native American peoples.

Spanish adventurers of the early 16th century were the first Europeans to explore the American coast of the Caribbean Sea. They claimed the American mainland for Spain, earning it the name the Spanish Main. Inland, the Spanish discovered great and wealthy civilizations: the Aztecs of Mexico and the Incas of Peru. The Spanish made these native Americans slaves, stole their wealth and loaded it on to ships for transport to Spain. Not all their loot arrived: as news of their fabulous treasures spread, pirates flocked to the region, to take the precious cargoes for themselves.

▾ **Spanish treasure ships:** vessels were safe so long as they travelled in convoys (large groups). Stragglers and ships blown off course in storms, however, were easy targets for pirates to pick off.

☠ SIR FRANCIS DRAKE

The English were the most enthusiastic raiders of Spanish treasure. The two nations were at war and regularly attacked each other's ships and towns. The English queen, Elizabeth I, encouraged mariners to attack the Spanish. Although they were called privateers, these daring adventurers were really licensed pirates. Francis Drake (1540–1596) was the most famous. In 1572 he raided the Spanish town of Nombre de Dios in Panama. Drake was wounded, but the raid was a brilliant success, making Drake a rich man and an English hero. It also earned him the hatred of the Spanish.

When Francis Drake raided the Spanish treasure ship *Cacafuego* in 1578, it took his crew four days to unload the precious cargo. In addition to 13 chests of silver coins, there were 26 tons of silver blocks, 80 pounds of gold and countless jewels and pearls. Drake took his rich prize back to England – he needed it to pay off the wealthy people who had backed him. Many 17th- and 18th-century pirates had no sponsors to pay off. Instead, they shared out their captured booty. Only the captain and a few other officers got double shares. This fair scheme made pirate crews as wealthy as today's lottery winners. If a pirate got lucky, his portion of the treasure from just one raid could amount to £5,000 – more than he could earn in 40 years in the navy.

▲ **Pirate hoards:** although some hoards could amount to many thousands of pounds, pirates were notorious for spending, rather than saving, their stolen pieces of silver and gold.

▲ **Inca gold:** the Spanish conquistadores (conquerors) melted down captured ornaments to make the precious metals easier to carry. The few pieces that have survived show the fantastic talent of Inca and Aztec goldsmiths and silversmiths.

In Vera Cruz on the Spanish Main
stands a pirate tough and bold.
He watches as the ships that dock
are loaded up with Aztec gold.
When darkness falls he slinks away,
thinking up a daring plot,
To raid the ship, enslave the crew,
to find the gold and steal the lot!

PIRACY BOOMS!

While European nations were at war there was plenty of work for lawless sea rogues. As soon as peace returned in the early 18th century, only piracy offered the thrills – and rewards – they had grown used to.

'North and South America are infested with the rogues!' exclaimed James Logan, governor of the Atlantic island of Bermuda, in 1717. It was hardly surprising: piracy had been booming since a peace treaty four years earlier had ended a long war in Europe. Many of the sailors who had been fighting in privateer ships and in the English navy had become pirates; 1,500 of them were cruising in the Caribbean and off the American coast.

The peace treaty was not the only cause of the pirate menace, however. Since about 1620, buccaneers had been raiding Spanish shipping and settlements in the Caribbean. The buccaneers' most daring exploit came 50 years later, when Welsh pirate Henry Morgan led a small army of

▲ **The Caribbean:** a region where piracy became big business during the 1700s.

them through Central American jungles to raid the Spanish city of Panama. The buccaneers operated from the island base of Tortuga, just north of Hispaniola, and later from the Jamaican town of Port Royal. When Jamaica's government cracked down on piracy in the late 17th century, the buccaneers looked farther afield. Some moved to the Bahamas, turning the island of New Providence, north of Cuba, into a pirate's haven.

The pirate spy rejoins his ship and tells his fellows what he's seen. Their eyes grow wide at tales of gold and with envy they turn green.

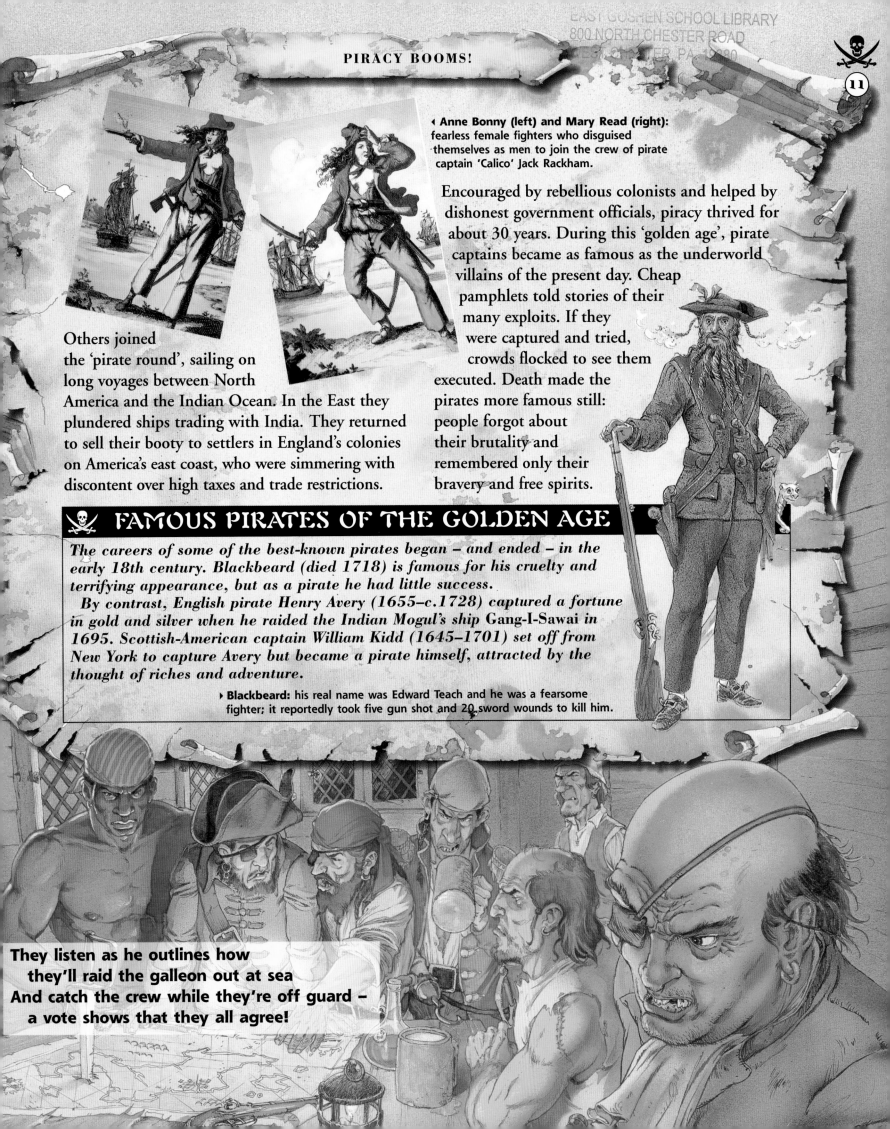

◄ **Anne Bonny (left) and Mary Read (right):** fearless female fighters who disguised themselves as men to join the crew of pirate captain 'Calico' Jack Rackham.

Encouraged by rebellious colonists and helped by dishonest government officials, piracy thrived for about 30 years. During this 'golden age', pirate captains became as famous as the underworld villains of the present day. Cheap pamphlets told stories of their many exploits. If they were captured and tried, crowds flocked to see them executed. Death made the pirates more famous still: people forgot about their brutality and remembered only their bravery and free spirits.

Others joined the 'pirate round', sailing on long voyages between North America and the Indian Ocean. In the East they plundered ships trading with India. They returned to sell their booty to settlers in England's colonies on America's east coast, who were simmering with discontent over high taxes and trade restrictions.

☠ FAMOUS PIRATES OF THE GOLDEN AGE

The careers of some of the best-known pirates began – and ended – in the early 18th century. Blackbeard (died 1718) is famous for his cruelty and terrifying appearance, but as a pirate he had little success.

By contrast, English pirate Henry Avery (1655–c.1728) captured a fortune in gold and silver when he raided the Indian Mogul's ship Gang-I-Sawai in 1695. Scottish-American captain William Kidd (1645–1701) set off from New York to capture Avery but became a pirate himself, attracted by the thought of riches and adventure.

▸ **Blackbeard:** his real name was Edward Teach and he was a fearsome fighter; it reportedly took five gun shot and 20 sword wounds to kill him.

They listen as he outlines how
they'll raid the galleon out at sea
And catch the crew while they're off guard –
a vote shows that they all agree!

THE PIRATE SHIP

Cutting through the ocean spray, a pirate sloop chases after a heavily-laden cargo ship. It's an unequal race which the sloop wins easily, as pirate vessels were some of the best ships at sea.

What qualities made a good pirate ship? Speed was the most important factor. Big ships with many large sails were generally faster than little ships with a few smaller sails. The shape of a ship's hull also affected its speed, and long, narrow hulls were quicker than short, fat ones.

Pirates choosing a ship also needed to know how close to the wind it could sail. This meant how far the helmsman could steer into the wind before the ship stopped moving. Ships with square sails needed the wind behind them to move through the waves, but those with sails rigged (arranged) from the front to the back of the ship were more flexible. These were called fore-and-aft rigged ships and could sail very quickly when the wind was coming from one side.

Ships with shallow drafts also had a crucial advantage. The draft of a ship is how much of its hull is underwater, and means the depth of water in which the ship can sail. Pirates sailing a ship with a shallow draft could lurk craftily in shallow coves or bays. If they were being chased by a navy ship with a deeper draft, they could escape by sailing across a sand-bar or reef where the other ship would run aground.

The 17th- and 18th-century pirates who cruised the Caribbean and American coasts found that two types of ships suited their needs best. Sloops built in Bermuda or Jamaica were small ships, usually having just one single mast. Most sails were rigged

▲ **Schooner:** a fast ship that could be handled with a small crew.

▲ **Sloop:** a ship with a large sail that spread from the long bowsprit at the front to give it extra speed.

In a secret sheltered creek
the ruffians beach their battered craft,
They clean the hull of shells and weed,
careening it from fore to aft.

▶ **Cutaway: a typical pirate ship**
1 Great cabin
2 Cargo stowed in hold
3 Captain's cabin
4 Master's cabin
5 Carpenter's cabin
6 Crewspace
7 Main hatch
8 Cannon
9 Windlass

for their own purpose. They might change the rigging – this is the arrangement of masts, sails and yards (the bars from which the sails hung). They would replace some of the square sails with fore-and-aft rigging, and perhaps lengthen the bowsprit (the sail-carrying spar that extends from the front of the ship).

To make the ship more menacing, they would add extra guns. The weight of cannons on the upper deck could make a ship unstable, so pirates usually fitted them on the lower deck.

They would take down internal partitions and create a single 'flush' deck running the whole length of the ship. To fire the guns they would cut gunports (square holes with doors to keep out the sea) in the ship's side.

For extra speed, pirates would careen their ship – scrape all the weed and barnacles from the hull. To do this they had to find a creek or shore with a steeply sloping beach of sand or shingle. Moored there at high tide, a ship would be left 'high and dry' when the tide went out. The crew could then scrape and repair the exposed hull until the tide rose again.

fore-and-aft, although one or two square topsails gave the ship extra speed in light winds. The schooner, like the ship shown above, was also fore-and-aft rigged, but had two masts instead of one.

If pirates captured a ship that was better than their own, they would adopt it and then adapt it

They rig new sails to speed their ship much faster through the ocean spray, And line the sides with cannons bright to boom a warning to their prey.

PIRATE WEAPONS

When pirates swarmed aboard a ship, they were ready to fight to the death with pistols, swords, daggers and axes. They expected no mercy, and they didn't spare the lives of sailors who resisted the attack.

Though pirate ships bristled with cannons, few crews had enough training to use these big guns effectively. Instead they relied on hand weapons, boarding victims' ships and capturing them in hand-to-hand battles. Every pirate packed several pistols, because they had to be reloaded after every shot. Since there was never time to do this, pirates either dropped the pistol after firing it, or used the gun as a club. Under pirate articles (see pages 18–19) that pirates signed on joining the crew, each was responsible for keeping his personal weapons cleaned and ready for action at all times.

▲ **Flintlock pistol:** this weapon was unreliable – it simply fizzled if the damp sea air moistened the powder inside.

▲ **Long knives:** not just used as a weapon, they had a thousand peaceful uses on board ship.

◄ **Cutlass:** a short sword with a wide, slightly curved blade. There wasn't room to swing a longer sword in cabins or on decks crowded with rigging.

▲ **Dagger:** easy to hide in a pocket, or to tuck into a belt.

◄ **Boarding axe:** used for cutting through the thick ropes that held up the rigging, bringing sails and spars crashing down to the deck.

A cannon could blast a heavy iron ball as far as 1.5 km (approx. 1 mile). They were much more frightening and dangerous at close range, though, so pirates waited until their target was directly alongside before firing.

Firing a cannon was not easy on dry land; on the rocking deck of a pirate ship it was even more difficult. The gun weighed as much as a modern car, and to move it, five or more pirates had to pull hard on ropes and levers. To load the gun and clean it after each shot, the crew had to stand in the gunport, where they made easy targets for an enemy sharpshooter. Finally, there was always the danger that a stray spark would set light to gunpowder before it was loaded, and blow everyone sky-high. In 1669, there was an accident on Henry Morgan's ship when the whole gunpowder store was blown up by one single gun.

▲ **Fire power:** firing a cannon took one man a second, but reloading it was heavy, dangerous work for a team of at least six. It's hardly surprising that pirate crews preferred to fire only one or two shots.

Because of all these difficulties, pirates more often used cannon fire not to sink the ship they were raiding, but to frighten the crew into submission. If this did not work, they fired chains to take down the sails, and grapeshot (small lumps of metal) to kill anyone left on deck.

Henry Avery was a master at using cannons to capture other ships. Avery preferred to aim at the sails and masts of his intended victim's ship, which disabled the vessel much more quickly than trying to sink it.

One of his most famous victories against the Mogul fleet in 1695 was won with the skilful use of over 60 cannons.

Loading and firing cannons wasn't just a job for grizzled old pirates, though. At just seven or eight years of age, boys were considered old enough to fetch and carry charges of gunpowder from the magazine (a protected store-room deep in the ship) to the guns on the decks above.

On board their ship, the *Lively Lass*,
    the pirate captain tells his crew:
'Spare no one's life when we attack;
    you can be sure they won't spare you.'
They sharpen up their knives and swords
    and load each gun with charge and ball.
Then armed and ready to attack,
    they dream they'll have a golden haul.

THE ATTACK

In story books, pirates attack with all guns blazing, then face a bloody fight to capture a victim's ship. In real life, pirate attacks were rather different – but just as frightening.

Pirates knew just how to terrify their victims. They threatened them with a row of cannons, and made themselves look as ferocious as they could. They crowded on to deck shouting blood-curdling curses, firing pistols and hurling smoke bombs. They overwhelmed their victims by sheer numbers, as pirate crews were six or seven times the size of the crews of the merchant (trading) ships on which they preyed. Sometimes just the threat of an attack was enough to make a ship surrender.

Pirates did not even need to threaten violence if they could take the crew by surprise. Ships at anchor were easy victims at night because only a few sailors kept watch. Pirates could row quietly across and capture the ship while most of the crew were sleeping.

▲ **The Jolly Roger:** this was every pirate ship's trademark, with each captain having his own individual design.

Some seamen even welcomed pirates aboard, for an attack could bring an improvement to the hardship of their lives at sea. The English writer Samuel Johnson described life on a ship as like 'being in jail, with the chance of being drowned', adding that there was more room, better food, and better company in prison.

Another common trick was to disguise the pirate ship as a peaceful merchant vessel. When they saw a potential target, most of the pirates hid themselves. The unarmed crew that remained on deck could then sail close to their victims without arousing suspicion. When they were near enough, they might ask a favour, perhaps saying they had run out of water. As soon as the sails of the two ships were touching, the rest of the pirates hoisted the Jolly Roger and emerged from hiding to claim their prize.

☠ THE JOLLY ROGER

The Jolly Roger, supposedly from the French phrase joli rouge, was the standard pirate flag and had a special meaning: it invited the crew under attack to give up their ship without a fight. If they didn't, the pirates replaced the Jolly Roger with a plain red flag which signalled that they would slaughter everyone without mercy. Story-book pirates decorated their black flags with a white skull and crossbones, and indeed pirate captain Henry Avery really did fly a flag just like this. There were countless other patterns, however. Besides skulls, bones and skeletons, pirates also used symbols such as swords and blood.

Jack Rackham

Thomas Tew

Henry Avery

Bartholomew Roberts

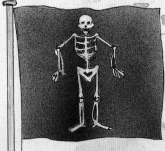

Edward Low

Edward England

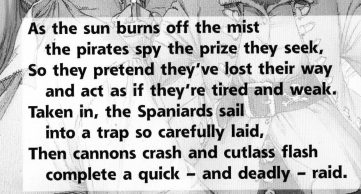

As the sun burns off the mist
  the pirates spy the prize they seek,
So they pretend they've lost their way
  and act as if they're tired and weak.
Taken in, the Spaniards sail
  into a trap so carefully laid,
Then cannons crash and cutlass flash
  complete a quick – and deadly – raid.

SHARING THE BOOTY

'Eleven hundred ounces gold; 2,353 ounces silver . . . rubies, small and great, sixty seven stones; four large diamonds set in lockets, and one large diamond set in a gold ring; sundry precious stones, rings, crystals, amethysts, gold ingots and gold dust.'

This was just part of the booty pirate captain William Kidd had hoarded by the time he was caught in 1699. His riches even kept him awake – he'd stuffed his mattress with gold bars! Kidd was not the most successful pirate, but he was greedier than most. He kept more than his fair share of the treasure he seized – 20 times as much as he gave each member of his crew.

Other pirate captains had to be more generous, because their pirate crews followed strict rules about dividing up the booty. The share-out was explained in detail in pirates' articles.

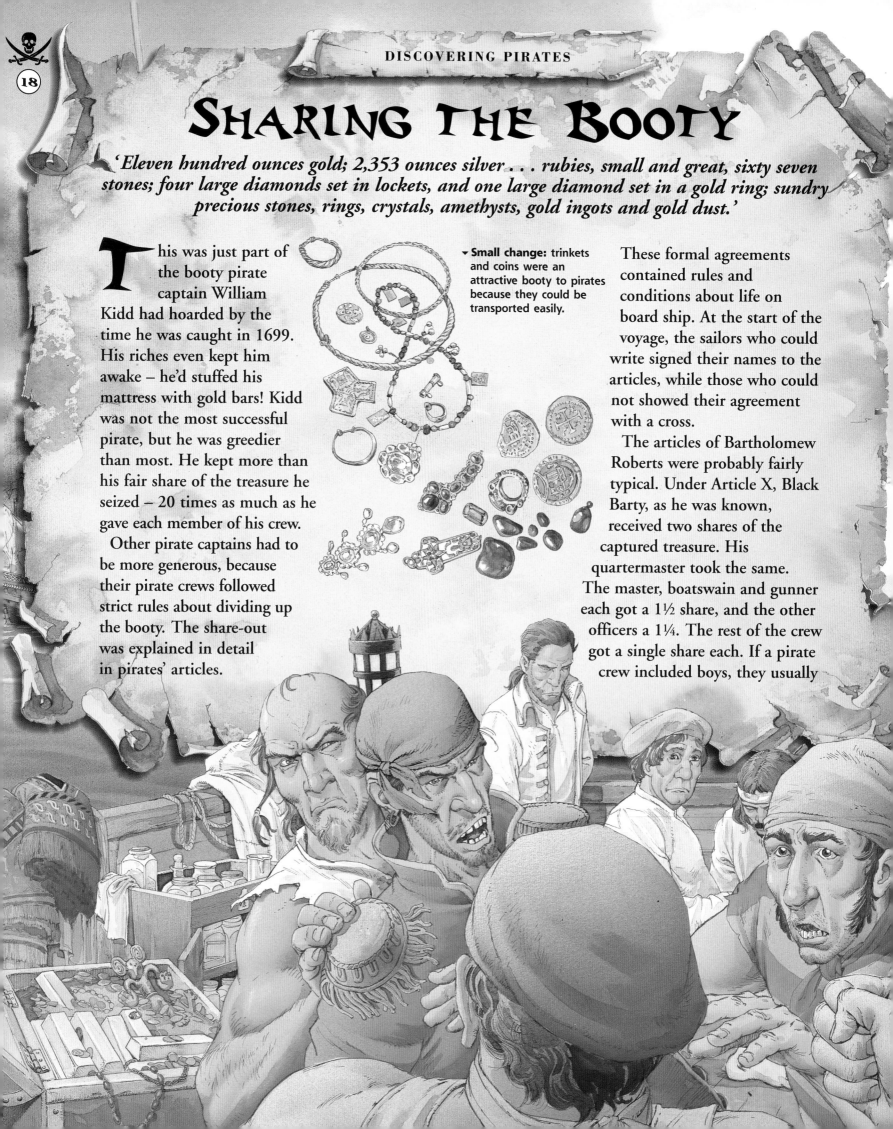

▶ **Small change:** trinkets and coins were an attractive booty to pirates because they could be transported easily.

These formal agreements contained rules and conditions about life on board ship. At the start of the voyage, the sailors who could write signed their names to the articles, while those who could not showed their agreement with a cross.

The articles of Bartholomew Roberts were probably fairly typical. Under Article X, Black Barty, as he was known, received two shares of the captured treasure. His quartermaster took the same. The master, boatswain and gunner each got a 1½ share, and the other officers a 1¼. The rest of the crew got a single share each. If a pirate crew included boys, they usually got a half share of the spoils or less. Even this could be a small fortune, though. When pirates led by Henry Avery raided the Indian ship *Gang-I-Sawai* in 1695, crew members between 16 and 18 years of age received £500 each. Younger boys got about £100 – roughly four year's wages for a skilled man of the time.

Before the booty was divided, those who had been wounded in its capture received special payments. Black Barty's crew got £800 if they had lost a leg or an arm. For lesser injuries, this pirate pension plan paid out smaller amounts.

If the pirates raided a ship carrying a chest of money, paying everyone off was easy – the captain just counted out the coins. This was unusual, though, as most cargoes were difficult

▲ **Snake eyes:** losing their share of treasure was far too easy for many pirates, as they gambled it away in games of cards and dice.

▲ **Inca statue:** the Aztec and Inca people in Central and South America were famed for their gold. Pirates wasted no time in replundering their wealth from the Spaniards.

or even impossible to divide, and arguments were common.

For example, when pirates seized a ship carrying diamonds in 1721, most of the crewmen received 42 precious gemstones each. A few diamonds were very much bigger and more valuable than the rest. One pirate got a single large stone of enormous value. Disappointed that he had fewer stones than his shipmates, he smashed it up into dozens of worthless splinters!

What did pirates do with their share of the booty? Few saved it – they saw little point. Most quickly spent their share on women, drinking and having a good time. Some were cheated of their wealth, especially if it was in a form they could not easily use for money, such as rolls of precious silk. Crooked traders exchanged their riches for rotten food and beds with bugs. Mostly though, pirates gambled away their wealth with cards and dice. In just three weeks during 1667, a pirate crew led by the French buccaneer L'Olonnais lost 260,000 pieces-of-eight. This was an enormous amount of money – at that time just two of the coins were enough to buy a whole cow!

To share the loot the captain takes
a very, very long, long time:
It isn't easy to divide
a ton of gold by 99!
Because they cannot be shared out
the bolts of silk are torn to shreds,
And everybody wears a hat
in blues and pinks, greens and reds.

A Terrible Fate

The 'Golden Age' of piracy was not so golden for those who fell into the pirates' clutches. Their captors were often violent and cruel, and the worst of them delighted in merciless torture and murder.

Pirates lived in violent times. On land, death by hanging was the punishment for all thieves. At sea, cruel captains flogged and tortured sailors who disobeyed orders. It's hardly surprising that pirates used violence to get what they wanted – or for revenge. Violence was a quick and simple way for pirates to discover everything about the ships they raided. Under threat of torture, most captains would lead their pirate captors to the most valuable cargo in the hold. Those who did not soon regretted their decision, for when faced with resistance, pirates showed little mercy.

Some were especially cruel, like Edward Low, who flew into a rage in

▲ **Pirate myth:** in reality, few pirates made their prisoners actually walk the plank, although they often pushed a few overboard.

1722 when a Portuguese captain dropped a bag of money into the sea, rather than hand it over. Low 'ordered the captain's lips to be cut off, which he broiled before his face' before killing him and his crew. French buccaneer François L'Olonnais was just as bloodthirsty. During a raid on the Caribbean coast in 1667, he tortured his prisoners to make them reveal a route to safety. He 'ripped open one of the prisoners with a cutlass, tore the living heart out of his body, gnawed at it, then hurled it at the face of one of the others, saying "show me the way, or I will do the same to you" '.

These monsters seemed to take horrible pleasure in devising ever

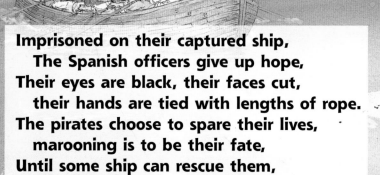

Imprisoned on their captured ship,
   The Spanish officers give up hope,
Their eyes are black, their faces cut,
   their hands are tied with lengths of rope.
The pirates choose to spare their lives,
   marooning is to be their fate,
Until some ship can rescue them,
   They face a long and lonely wait.

more ingenious tortures. Few other pirates were as cruel, but beating or wounding captives was routine. Drinking may have made pirates more angry and quarrelsome. Most ships carried large stocks of rum, brandy or other strong drinks and pirate crews drank themselves senseless at every opportunity. Piracy itself also made men desperate. Since they could expect some form of horrible punishment if they were caught, pirates took every precaution – including murder – to avoid capture.
One of the more humane pirate punishments was marooning. Captives were put ashore on an uninhabited island, and left to fend for themselves. To make life less tough, the castaways were given a little water and food, and a gun and ammunition to shoot game. Marooning takes its name from a Spanish word, *cimarron*, meaning wild or untamed.
No pirate story would be complete without someone 'walking the plank'. In this cruel drowning game, pirates blindfolded their captives and tied their hands. The prisoners were then forced to walk off the end of a plank extended over the sea from the side of the ship. There are no reliable records of 17th- and 18th-century pirates punishing their victims this way, however. This myth was popular in the 19th century and may have been based on old stories of Turkish pirates in the Mediterranean Sea who 'released' their captives and told them they were free to walk home – across the sea!

▲ **Left for dead:** leaving prisoners abandoned on remote islands was commonplace. It was also a punishment for any pirates caught stealing from their fellow crew members.

◄ **Cat o'nine tails:** victims often had to make their own 'temporary' whips before being flogged with them by merciless pirates. The whip was thrown overboard after use to avoid the risk of any infection spreading.

▶ **Marooning kit:** prisoners got a little gunpowder – probably in a special container made of animal horn – and a pistol or musket for shooting game.

SAILING FOR HOME

Without accurate charts (sea maps) and using only the simplest of instruments, pirates sailed the world's oceans in search of treasure. How did they manage it?

If you have ever used a map to travel to a place you have never been before, you will know how hard it can be to find your way on land. At sea, navigation is doubly difficult. Because the Earth's surface is curved, distant objects seem to sink beneath the waves as you sail away from them. Once a ship is a couple of hours from port, there's nothing to see but the sea.

Pirates found their way around this world of water in the same way as other seamen of their time – with a few simple instruments and lots of experience. When these failed, they relied on luck and prayers!

The ship's captain or master was in charge of navigation. His most important instrument was a compass. Its magnetic needle always pointed north, no matter which way the ship headed. Markings around the outside of the compass showed the ship's direction.

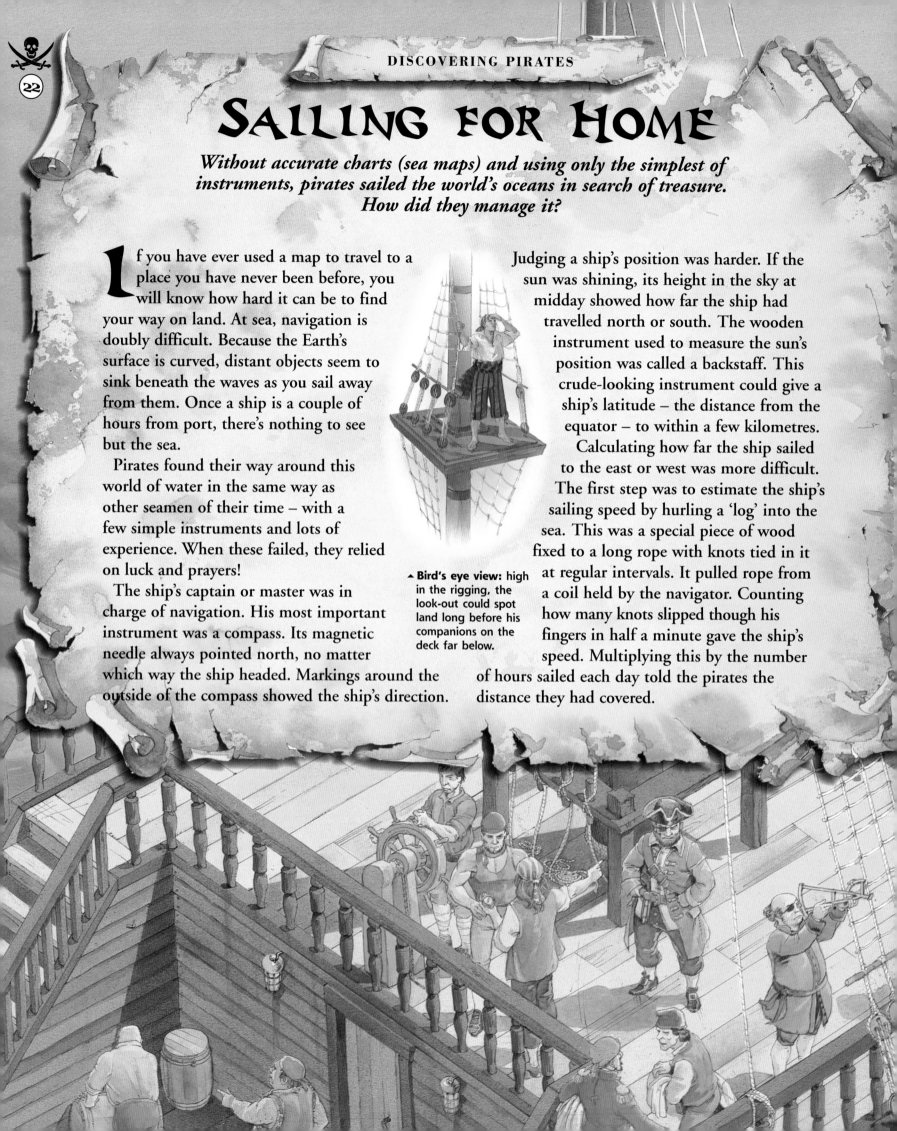

▲ **Bird's eye view:** high in the rigging, the look-out could spot land long before his companions on the deck far below.

Judging a ship's position was harder. If the sun was shining, its height in the sky at midday showed how far the ship had travelled north or south. The wooden instrument used to measure the sun's position was called a backstaff. This crude-looking instrument could give a ship's latitude – the distance from the equator – to within a few kilometres.

Calculating how far the ship sailed to the east or west was more difficult. The first step was to estimate the ship's sailing speed by hurling a 'log' into the sea. This was a special piece of wood fixed to a long rope with knots tied in it at regular intervals. It pulled rope from a coil held by the navigator. Counting how many knots slipped though his fingers in half a minute gave the ship's speed. Multiplying this by the number of hours sailed each day told the pirates the distance they had covered.

A pirate ship could sail almost anywhere with a compass, a backstaff and a log – and a clever captain or master. Buccaneer explorer William Dampier was one of the best. He sailed round the world, and the book he wrote about his journey became a best-seller in 1697.

Not all pirates were as skilled at navigation as Dampier, though. Some 20 years after Dampier's famous voyage, English pirate William Kennedy wrecked his ship *Rover* on the coast of Scotland. He had discovered – too late – that nobody on board the *Rover* had the slightest idea how to use the ship's instruments!

Much of the coast of Europe had been mapped by the start of the 18th century, but pirates in the Caribbean had no detailed printed charts to guide them on their way, unless they managed to find one among any stolen cargoes. Instead they relied on books of sailing directions, called ruttiers, portolans or waggoners. These hand-written pilot books were cherished by navigators. In them they recorded safe routes around dangerous headlands, and sketched the coastline on the approach to harbours.

▲ **Compass**

▼ **Backstaff**

▲ **Lost at sea:** fantasy treasure maps like this one wouldn't help pirates avoid a shipwreck! Proper sea charts, however, marked shallow water, dangerous rocks and good places to anchor.

Setting off to journey homeward
cheers up every buccaneer,
But on this ship of shared decisions
they can't agree which course to steer.
'North by north-west' says the captain,
'Steer to starboard' calls the mate,
The master laughs at their opinions
for only he can navigate.

HARDSHIPS AND HAZARDS

The life of an 18th-century pirate was in many ways similar to the life of an honest sailor of the time. Both suffered the same rotten food and ran the same risks of drowning, injury and disease.

Pirates had an easy life compared to other sailors. They shared the work of sailing their ship among a much larger crew; they stood the chance of becoming very rich very quickly; and if they did wrong, they weren't punished with the same cruelty as sailors on merchant or naval ships. In all other ways, pirates and honest seamen suffered just the same hardships and hazards.

A sailing ship was a dangerous place. Even in good weather the day-to-day routine forced the crew to take enormous risks. To work the sails they had to climb a swaying mast as high as any tree, and lift heavy, wet sheets of canvas. Few survived a fall to the deck. Those who did often lost an arm or a leg.

▲ **Ship duties:** jobs aboard ship were varied; provisioning a ship, while a heavy-duty and boring task, was also an important one. These stocks would see the crew through many weeks, even months, of sailing.

Pirates who slipped from the yardarm into the sea rarely survived. Even if their companions saw them fall, there was little they could do, as sailing ships don't have brakes like a car. Before you could shout 'man overboard!' the ship would have left the unfortunate pirate far behind. A search in the ship's boat was usually pointless, because even the smallest ocean waves were big enough to hide the bobbing head of a drowning shipmate.

Storms made the ocean even more deadly, and good sailors did all they could to avoid them. They did not put to sea in the stormiest seasons, and could recognize patterns of clouds that warned of approaching danger.

Pirates' weather-forecasting skills were of little use, however, if they were far from a safe port. When the storm hit, the best they could do was to turn the ship to face the wind, and wait until the weather improved.

Disease could kill as quickly and effectively as a shipwreck, and hit pirate and naval ships alike. In 1697, 30 members of William Kidd's crew died of tropical diseases in the time it took to careen their ship. When an English navy squadron visited the Caribbean to hunt pirates 30 years later, 4,000 sailors died of disease in two years, leaving only 750 survivors.

Many other hardships simply made life uncomfortable or unpleasant. Washing and doing laundry were difficult, and when pirates attacked a ship, they often exchanged the clothes of the crew for their own stinking rags. When fresh food ran out, the crew survived mostly on salted meat, dried peas and beans, cheese and 'bread', which was actually more like hard biscuits, often riddled with maggots. Even the most skilled cook could not make

◄ Stormy seas: the damage that even a small gale could do to a ship was devastating, often leaving the crew stranded on a remote island while they tried to repair their vessel as best they could.

an enjoyable meal from these poor ingredients, so whenever they reached land, pirates became hunters to secure a decent meal. Turtles were a favourite target for a tasty meal, as they were slow and easy to catch on land, and their meat added welcome variety to a sailor's rather predictable menu.

On long ocean journeys boredom was as hard to avoid as worms in a biscuit. Pirates fought it by gambling, getting drunk, or just talking – perhaps about how best to spend the booty from their next daring raid!

The sky grows black – a storm's ahead,
 there are no stars to steer by.
The mast is snapped, and crashing waves
 warn that rocks lurk nearby.
Washed up on a remote beach,
 the crew escape a watery grave,
And though their ship has run aground,
 at least their treasure they can save.

Treasure Island

A deserted island, a sandy shore, and an old stained map with an X marking where to dig. Is it just an exciting story, or is there buried pirates' treasure still to be found?

Washed up on the beach of a deserted tropical island, the last thing pirates had on their mind was burying treasure. Instead, they probably first did what island visitors have done ever since: they had a barbecue. For these castaways, outdoor cooking wasn't just a change from hotel food. It was the only way to eat. There was no shortage of things to cook on the coals. Fish and birds were easy to spear or shoot. Some islands were overrun by tame pigs and goats – the offspring of animals released by earlier visitors.

Water would not have been difficult to find, either, as all but the smallest islands have springs. In fact, for pirate castaways, the problem was likely to be too much water rather than too little, as tropical rain falls in torrents.

But after they had found food, drink and shelter, surely *then* pirates would have buried their treasure? Some certainly did – though the ones we know about didn't hide it on desert islands. When Francis Drake raided the Spanish town of Nombre de Dios in 1572, he briefly hid his plunder underground on the Central American coast. William Kidd really did

▲ **Cave of wealth:** Captain Kidd overseeing the burying of some of his pirate treasure in a well-hidden cave.

Hunger soon attacks the pirates,
  they search in vain for fish and fruits,
All they find is ocean turtles
  which taste just like their old sea boots.
To keep their treasure safely hidden
  they dig a pit both wide and deep,
They lower chests in to the bottom
  then pile the soil back in a heap.

bury his treasure on an island, but it wasn't tropical, nor was it uninhabited. Kidd chose Gardiners' Island, off the eastern tip of New York's Long Island. It was 1699, and Kidd was on the run. He knew it wouldn't be long before he was captured and tried for piracy. Cruising off the Long Island coast, Kidd landed on Gardiners' Island several times, and according to legend, buried at least some of his treasure there. Before Kidd was

hanged for piracy, £14,000 worth of his plunder was discovered – a fraction of the £400,000 he had looted from the ships he captured. The rest of Kidd's treasure was never found. Some of it may still be buried on Gardiners' Island. Maybe there is more hidden on the Caribbean islands Kidd visited on his way north? And perhaps he really did record where it was with an X on a wrinkled parchment map. We may never know.

LIFE OF A REAL CASTAWAY

The best known castaway of all was Robinson Crusoe, a character created in 1719 by English author Daniel Defoe. Defoe's book, Robinson Crusoe, describes how Crusoe was shipwrecked and survived for 24 years on an island before being rescued.

Defoe based his story on a real-life castaway called Alexander Selkirk (1676–1721). This Scottish sailor was not actually shipwrecked but he was a privateer – a kind of pirate. He asked to be put ashore on the island of Más á Tierra, 640 km (400 miles) west of Chile, South America, after quarrelling with his ship-mates.

Selkirk's survival instincts were amazing, and he lived on the island for five years, killing and eating wild goats and making clothes from their skins. When he was rescued in 1709, Selkirk looked like a wild man: his hair and beard had grown long, and he had almost forgotten how to speak.

THE CAPTURE!

Piracy had grown from a minor nuisance to a major menace. Something had to be done, and in 1718 it was. The English navy set out to track down Blackbeard, and pirates everywhere knew their Golden Age was coming to an end.

When long wars in Europe ended in 1713, thousands of sailors left the navy and joined pirate crews. But the return of peace also made life more difficult for the pirates. Without wars to fight, the English navy became the police of the seas.

One of their first targets was Blackbeard, but before long they had pirates on the run everywhere. Squadrons of heavily armed ships were patrolling in the four pirate hot-spots: off the coast of England's American colonies, in the Caribbean, off Africa's east coast, and in the Indian Ocean.

While the navy closed its net around pirates at sea, changes on land were also making their wicked trade more difficult. The most important change was an 'Act for the more Effectual Suppression of Piracy'. This new law made it easier to punish pirates. Instead of returning to England for trial, pirates could be tried wherever they committed their crimes, and punished on the spot.

The law also discouraged sailors from joining the pirates by introducing rewards for seamen who resisted pirate attack or who captured pirates. Captains of merchant ships could get licences to track down pirate ships, just like the navy.

The clamp-down brought rapid success. The pirates' small ships were no match for the immense floating fortresses of the English navy. The number of North American pirates dropped from about 2,000 in 1720 to half that number in just three years. There were only 200 by 1726. The number of pirate attacks fell sharply too – from around 50 in 1718, to just six in 1726.

◂ **British attack:** determined to wipe out piracy in the 18th century, the Navy set sail in the fastest ships, proudly sailing the British flag.

Ship ahoy! But what's that flag?
    its colours are red, white and blue.
If this is the British Navy
    they're here for battle, not rescue.
The ship sails in with all guns blazing,
    Our pirates may be brave and bold
But they can not defeat the Navy;
    soon they're chained up in the hold.

☠ BLACKBEARD'S LAST STAND

The hunt for the infamous pirate Blackbeard began in 1718, when Lieutenant Robert Maynard sailed after him with 60 men in two sloops. Blackbeard had moored his sloop, the Adventure, in shallow waters near Ocracoke Island, off North Carolina's coast. When Maynard attacked at dawn, Blackbeard cut his anchor cable and tried to escape. With no wind to fill the sails, however, his men had to row the ship. Maynard's ships gave chase, but ran aground.

Blackbeard, who had been drinking all night, appeared on deck and toasted Maynard, calling his men 'cowardly puppies'. But by now the rising tide was refloating the English ships, and they rowed ever nearer to the Adventure.

As they closed in, Blackbeard fired his cannons, killing six English men. At this, Maynard sent his crew out of sight. Only two remained on deck. The trick worked: Blackbeard thought his cannons had killed everyone, and when the ships drew alongside, he led his crew aboard the English ship.

The navy men sprang from hiding, and in the battle that followed Maynard and Blackbeard fought hand-to-hand. Five bullets hit the pirate chief, but he fought on until a Scottish sailor wounded his neck with a sword. When the pirate called, 'Well done, lad,' the Scotsman replied: 'If it be not well done, I'll do it better.' And with his second stroke, he cut Blackbeard's head clean off.

When the battle ended, Maynard kept the bearded head as a grisly trophy, and threw the body overboard. According to legend, it swam twice around the ship before sinking!

A Pirate's Punishment

For pirates who were caught red-handed, the future was grim. Tried and found guilty, they were sure to die on the gallows, close to the sea where they committed their evil crimes.

Few pirates were famous while they lived, but every pirate was a celebrity for a day if he was executed. Executions in the 18th century were as popular as any concert is today. Huge crowds gathered to watch the condemned pirate 'dance the hempen jig' – a grisly joke about prisoners' dying movements at the end of the hangman's hemp rope.

First, pirates had to be caught and tried, and this wasn't always easy. Until 1700, any pirates who committed crimes in seas patrolled by the English navy had to be tried and executed in England. This sometimes meant transporting prisoners across thousands of miles of ocean to stand trial. If they were found guilty, only the citizens of London watched them die. It would have been

▲ **Ankle fetters:** once captured, pirates were given no chance to escape.

▲ **Wooden gallows:** these were the most popular form of punishment for pirates in the 17th and 18th centuries.

far better, of course, if trials and executions could take place nearer the scene of the crime. There other sailors could watch – and think twice about taking up the evil trade. A change in the law eventually made this possible, and local courts far from England began to try and punish pirates. The trials were quick, but hardly fair.

▲ **Gibbet cage:** when he was captured in 1701, Captain Kidd had the misfortune to end his days in one of these gruesome iron cages.

Most pirates were uneducated sailors who could neither afford to employ a lawyer, nor knew how to defend themselves. A few escaped execution by pleading that they had been forced into

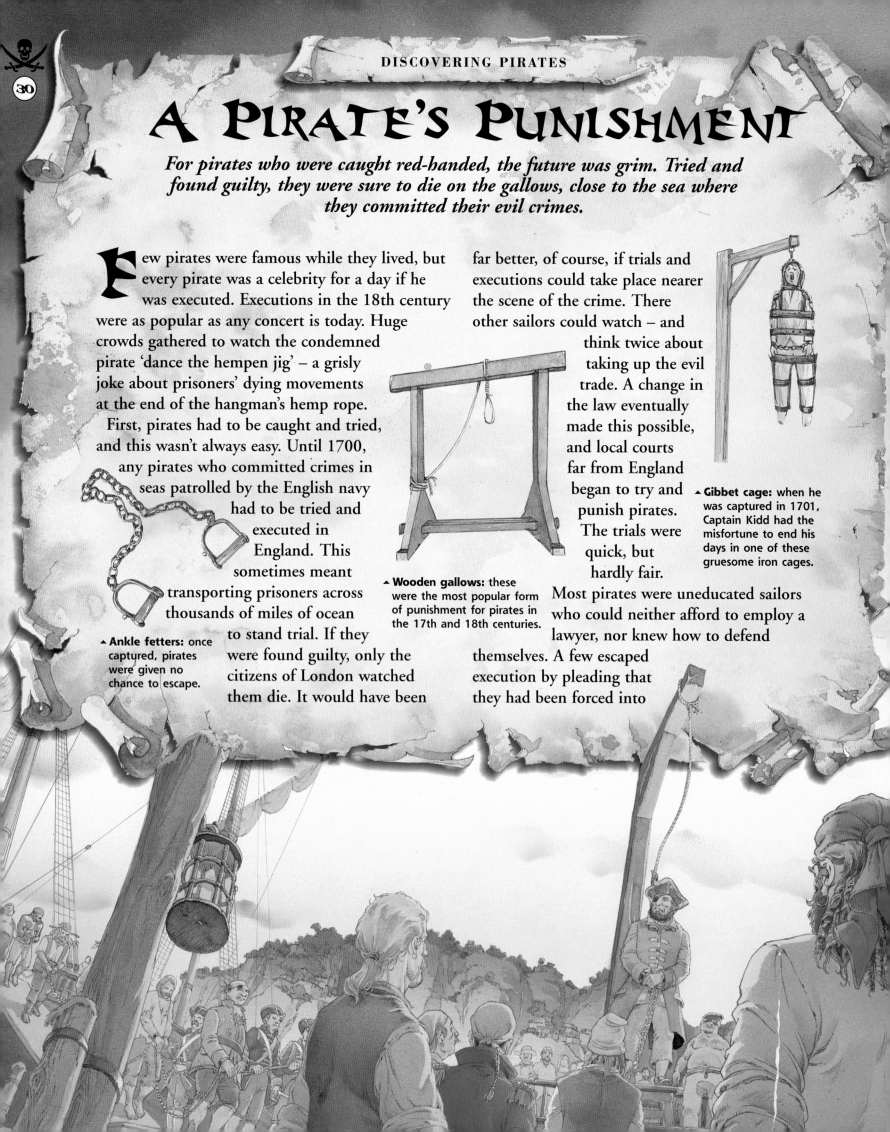

☠ AMNESTIES FOR PIRATES

During an amnesty, pirates who surrendered and swore never to return to their illegal ways received a pardon – their crimes were forgiven (if not forgotten). The best known was the Act of Grace which England's King George I proclaimed in 1717. He pardoned pirates who gave themselves up to the governors of England's colonies in America and the Caribbean. Not all the governors were convinced amnesties worked. One commented that: 'I don't perceive His Majesty's gracious proclamation of pardon works any good effect upon them, some few indeed surrender and take a certificate of doing so, and then several of them return to the sport again.'

THE
TRYALS
OF
Captain John Rackam,
AND OTHER
PIRATES, *Viz.*

George Fetherston,   Noah Harwood,
Richard Corner,   James Dobbins,
John Davies,   Patrick Carty,
John Howell,   Thomas Earl,
Tho. Bourn, *alias* Brown, John Fenwick, *or* Fenis

Who were all Condemn'd for PIRACY, at the Town of St. Jago de la Vega, in the Island of JAMAICA, on Wednesday and Thursday the Sixteenth and Seventeenth Days of November 1720.

AS ALSO, THE
TRYALS of Mary Read and Anne Bonny, *alias* Bonn, on Monday the 28th Day of the said Month of November, at St. Jago de la Vega aforesaid.

And of several Others, who were also condemn'd for PIRACY.

ALSO,
A True Copy of the Act of Parliament made for the more effectual Suppression...

Jamaica: Printed by Robert Baldwin, in the Year...

piracy. Some were more ingenious: Mary Read and Anne Bonny avoided the gallows by claiming they were pregnant.

Pirates who were found guilty were executed by hanging from a rope tied to a wooden gallows. To remind everyone that a pirate's crimes took place at sea, the gallows were set up on the sea-shore below high water. Death could be slow and painful, and friends sometimes cut short the suffering by pulling on the pirate's legs. The body was not cut down immediately but was left swinging from the gallows until three tides had washed over it.

For an unlucky few, the punishment continued, with 'hanging in chains'. The pirate's corpse was displayed on a gibbet (a wooden frame) inside an iron cage shaped like a suit of clothes. The 'gibbet chains' served a dual purpose – they stopped friends and relatives from stealing the body and giving it a decent burial, and they held together the pirate's rotting bones for a long-lasting spectacle. As an added preservative, the corpses were often covered in tar.

Peering through a tiny port-hole
the captain sees someone he knows.
Hanging dead, upon the quay side
a body left to decompose.
The judge finds all the pirates guilty –
will they hang like the captain's friend?
But no! They get a royal pardon –
our story has a happy end.

INDEX

A

Adventure, 29
Aegean Sea, 7
Africa, 28
America, 8, 11, 12, 27, 28, 31
amnesty, 31
ankle fetters, 30
articles, 14, 18–19
Assyrian galley, 6
Athenian drinking bowl, 7
Avery, Henry, 11, 16, 19
  flag, 17
Aztec, 8, 9

B

backstaff, 23
Bahamas, 10
Barbary coast, 6
Bermuda, 10, 13
Black Barty, 19
Blackbeard, 11, 14
  last stand, 29
boarding axe, 14
Bonny, Anne, 11, 31
boucan, 7
buccaneer, 7, 10

C

Cacafuego, 9
Caesar, Julius, 7
cannon, 14, 15, 16
careen, 13
Caribbean, 7, 8, 10, 12, 23, 25, 28, 31
castaway, 26-7
cat o'nine tails, 21
charts, 22–23
Chile, 27
compass, 22–23
Corsair, 6
Crusoe, Robinson, 27
cutlass, 14

D

dagger, 14
Dampier, William, 23
disease, 25
Dominican Republic, 7
Drake, Francis, 8, 9, 26
drowning, 21, 24

E

England, Edward, flag, 17
Elizabeth I, 8

F

flag, Jolly Roger, 16
food, 25, 26–7
fore-and-aft, 12–13

G

gallows, 30
Gang-I-Sawai, 11, 19
Gardiners' Island, 27
George I, 31
gibbet cage, 31
Greece, 6

H

Haiti, 7
hanging, 28, 30–1
Hispaniola, 7, 10

I

Inca, 8, 9, 19
India, 11
Indian Ocean, 10, 28

J

Jamaica, 10, 12
Jolly Roger, 16–17
Julius Caesar, 7

K

Kennedy, William, 23
Kidd, William, 11, 18, 25, 26–27

L

log, 22
Logan, James, 10
L'Olonnais, François, 19, 20
Long Island, 27
Low, Edward, 20
  flag, 17

M

maps, 23
marooning, 21
Más á Tierra, 27
Maynard, Robert, 29
Mediterranean Sea, 6–7
Mexico, 8
Mogul fleet, 11, 15
Morgan, Henry, 10, 15

N

navigation, 22
New Providence, 10

New York, 11, 27
Nombre de Dios, 8, 26
North Africa, 6
North Sea, 7

O

Ocracoke Island, 29

P

Panama, 8, 10
Peru, 8
pistol, flintlock, 14
Port Royal, 10
portolan, 22
Portugal, 20

R

Rackham, 'Calico' Jack, 11
  flag, 17
Read, Mary, 11, 30
red bones flag, 17
rigging, 12–13
Roberts, Bartholomew, 18, 19
  flag, 17
Robinson Crusoe, 27
Romans, 7
Rover, 23
ruttier, 23

S

Scandinavia, 7
schooner, 12
Selkirk, Alexander, 27
ship, design, 12
slavery, 8
sloop, 12
Spain, 7, 8, 9, 27
storms, 24–25

T

Teach, Edward, 11, 14
Tew, Thomas, flag, 17
Tortuga, 10
treasure, 8, 9, 18, 19, 27
Turkey, 7, 21

V

Vikings, 7

W

waggoner, 23
walking the plank, 21
weapons, 14–15